My Class

Vicky Braidich

REAL LIFE readers™

Rosen Classroom™

New York

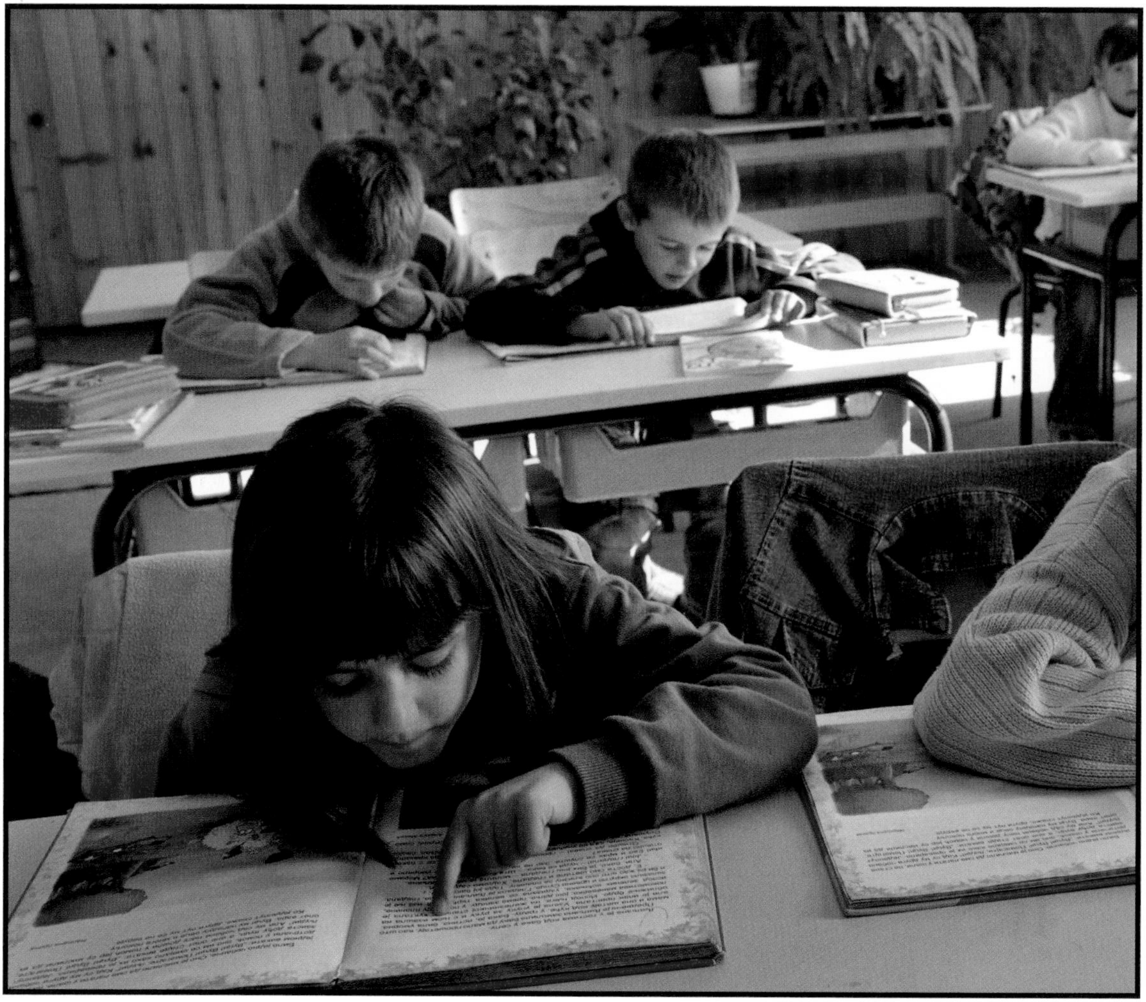

We read.

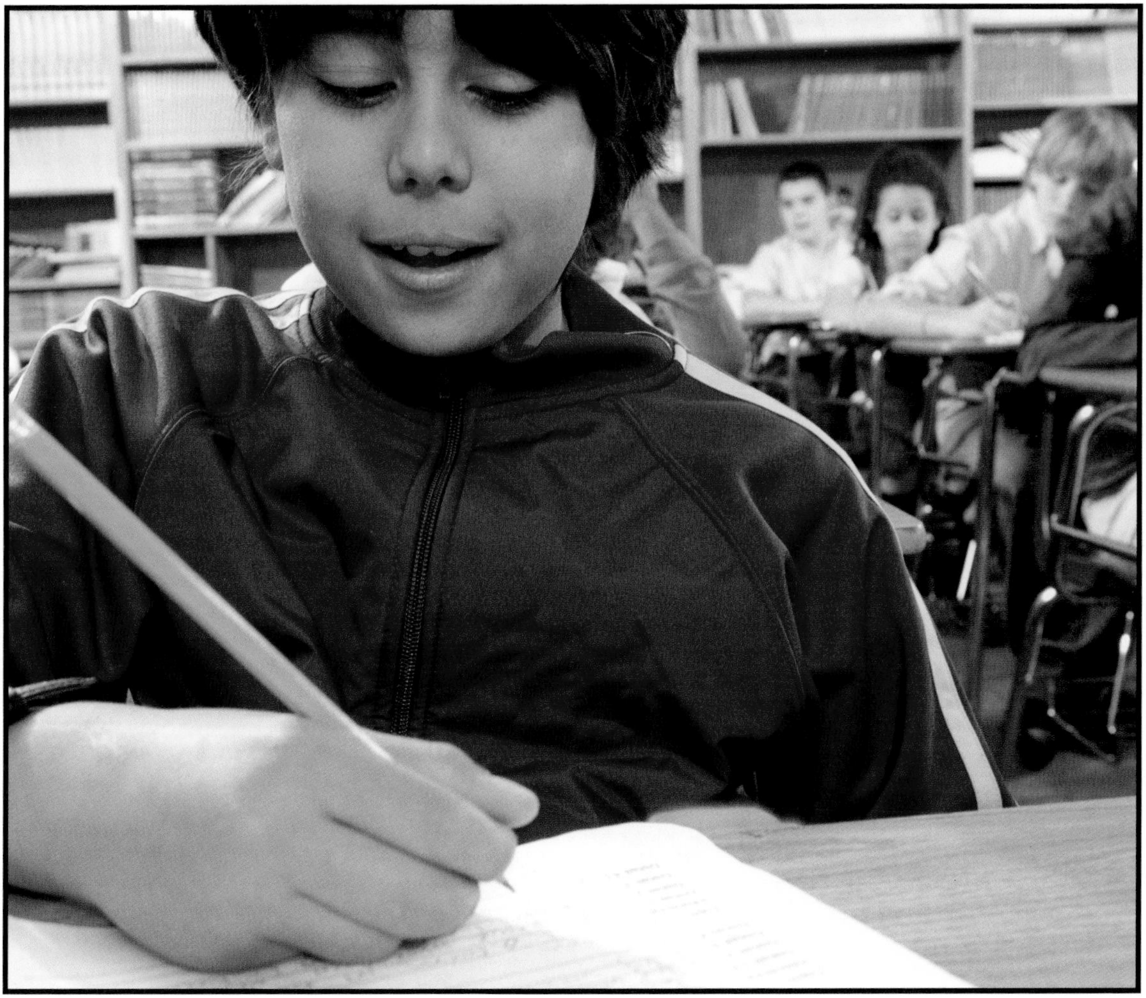

We write.

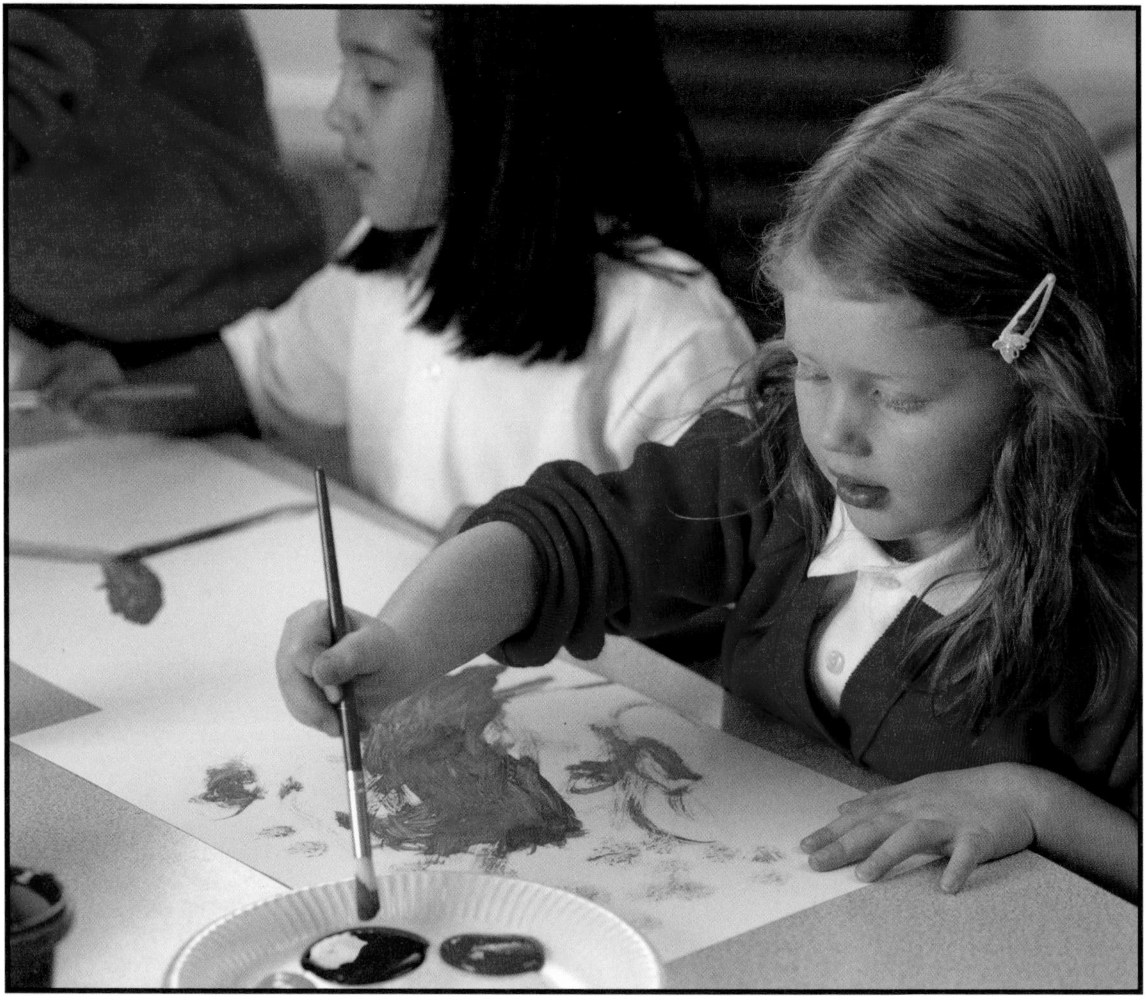

We paint.

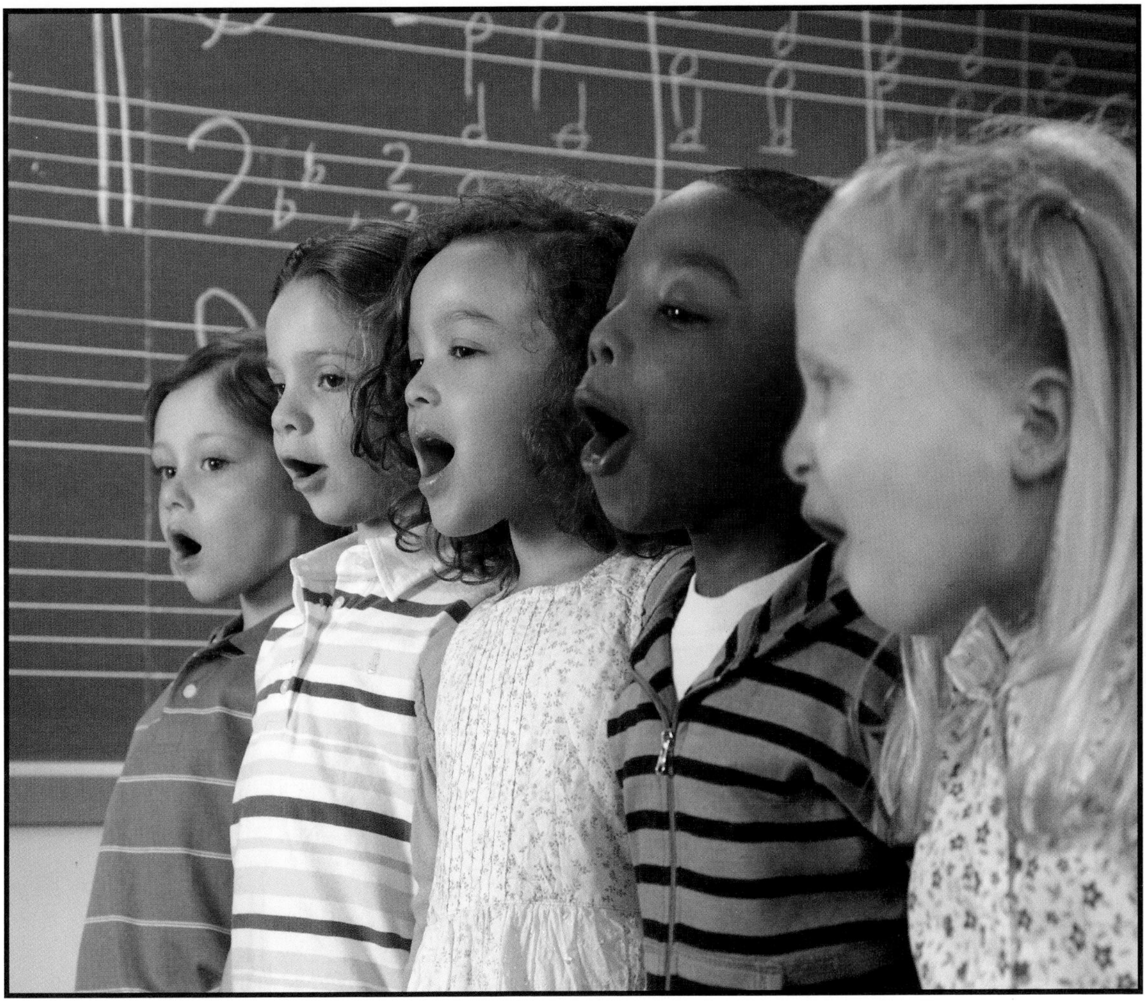

We sing.

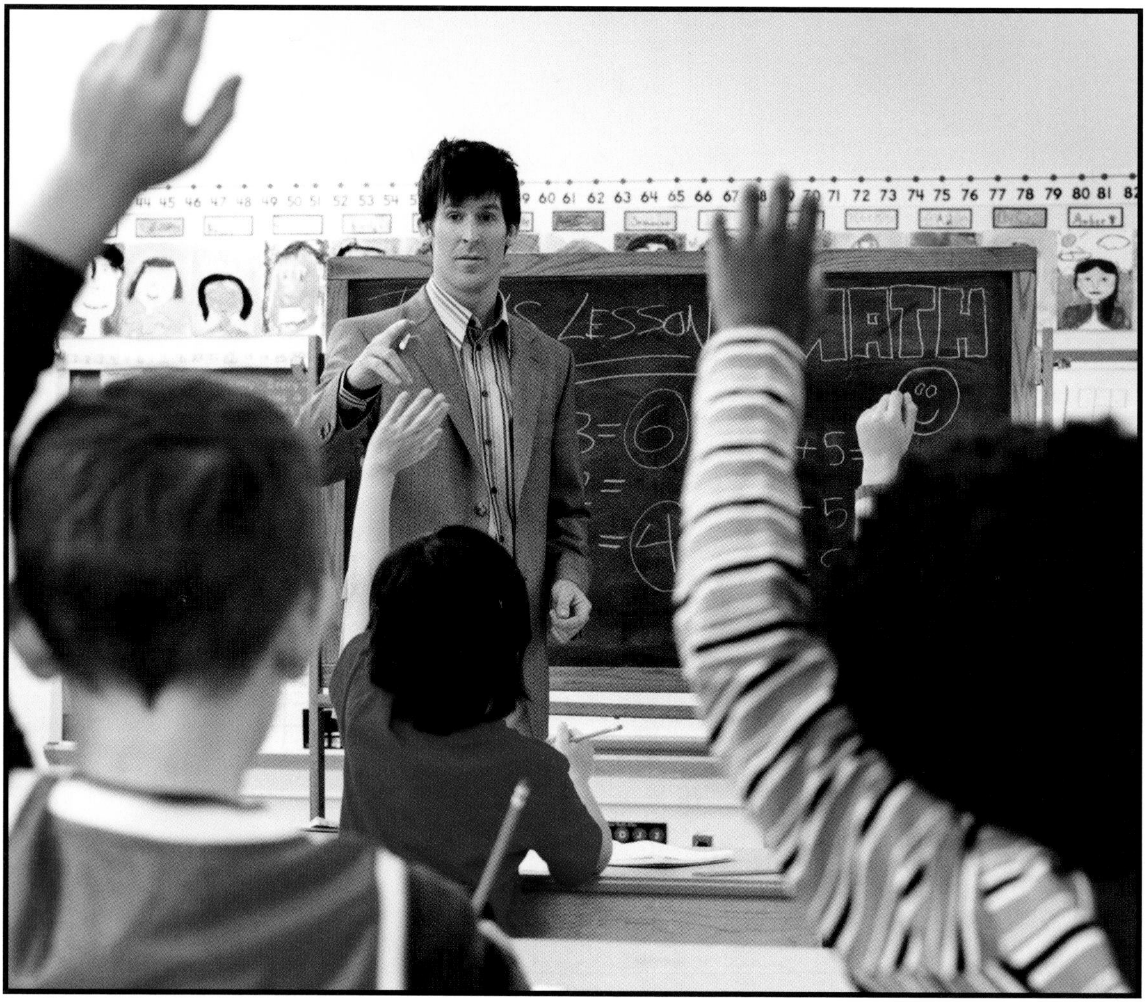

We like to learn.

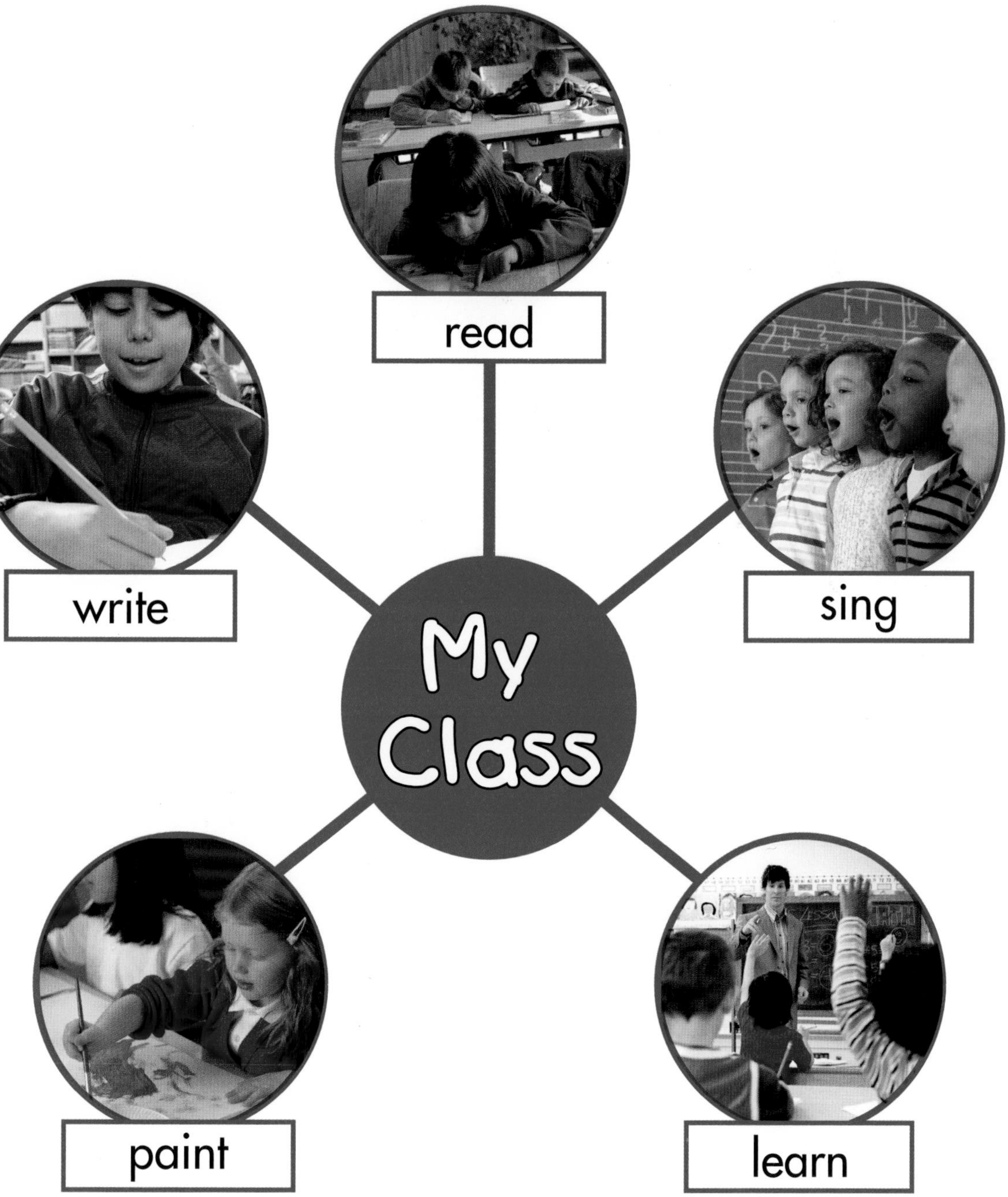
My Class
read
write
sing
paint
learn

Words to Know

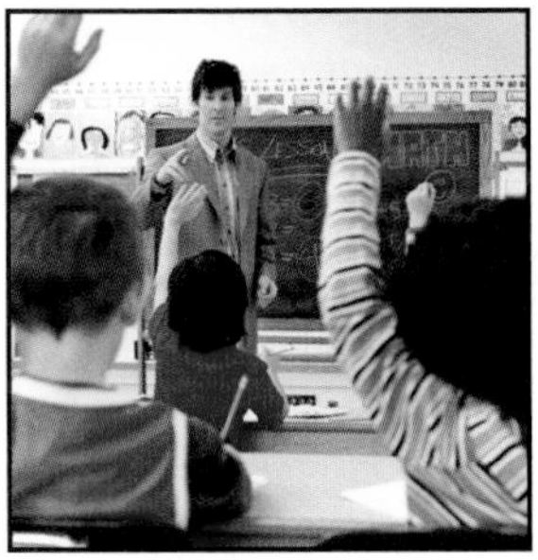

learn

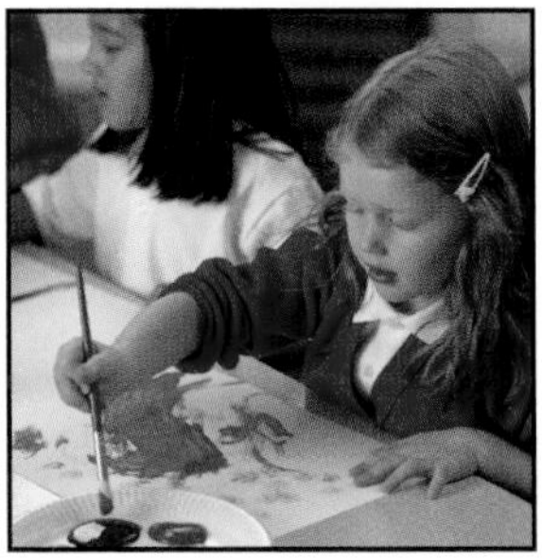

paint

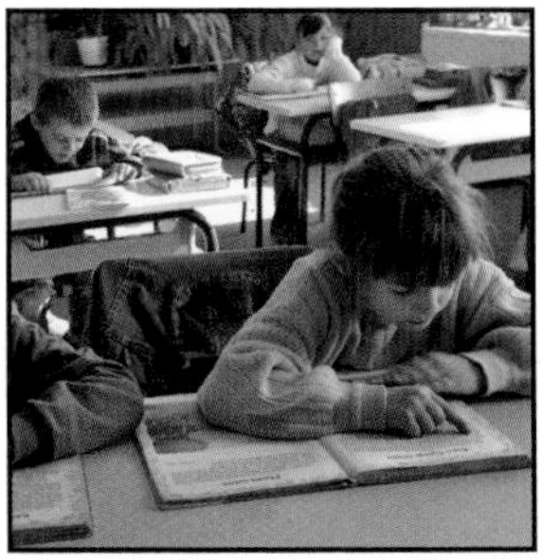

read

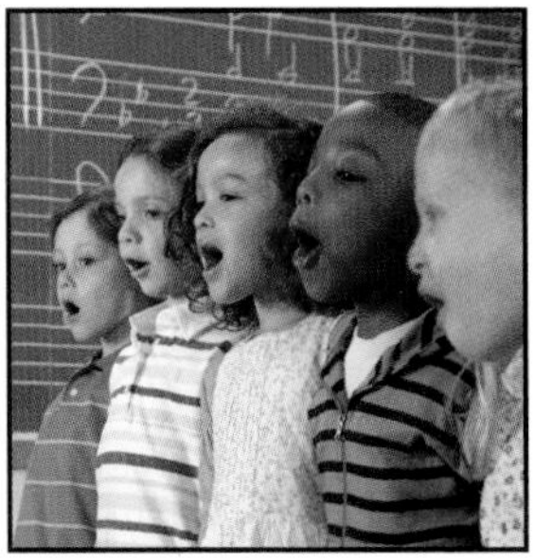

sing

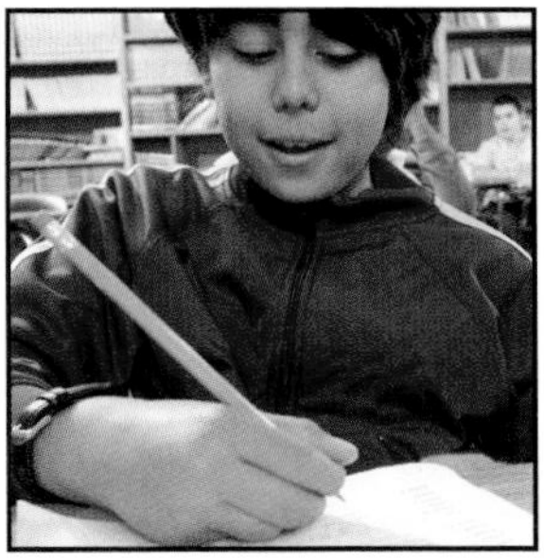

write